Legal Notice

© 2020

Damir Edenhofer

Müllerweg 91 - 64850 Schaafheim

First edition

Job Finder

In search of the right job for me

Contents

Prologue

This book is intended to serve you as a decision-making aid, primarily to create a new consciousness or to expand on what already exists. It will also show you how to combine your strengths and your personality with your interests in order to find the ideal profession for you.

In this book, I share with you, among other things, experiences that we as parents have had with our children, but also experiences that I have been able to gather during my long professional career. In the ideal case, this decision aid will make you more flexible in your thoughts. Moreover, it should encourage you to think more around corners and it should serve as a good signpost that helps you to look for and find a suitable job for you. No matter if you are looking for your first apprenticeship or if you have already gained some work experience, if you want to break out of unemployment or if you just want to change your job. Even if you should have other reasons and are looking for suitable jobs for yourself or others, this decision maker can help you in your search.

Briefly about my career: first apprenticeship at the end of the 80s - car mechanic (IHK), letter carrier, warehouse manager, environmental protection officer, sales inspector, second apprenticeship in 2010 as computer scientist (IHK), database developer, database administrator, sales representative IT security, overall responsibility for order process, distance learning to become a certified computer scientist (SGD), clerk, refugee assistance, system integrator, project manager, support, self-employed.

Meanwhile I am in my mid-forties and as you can see from my career, I have already worked in several different professions and fields of activity. The individual fields of activity are again very different and range from simple tasks, project management, management positions with over 100+ employees, to distance learning and self-employment. From this colourful mix and many other aspects, I would like to share my experiences with you.

Enjoy reading.

Then vs. now

The stories of friends and acquaintances made me often realise that certain problems that arise when choosing a profession are always the same or at least quite similar. Especially the young adolescents are confronted again and again with the question of what they want to become or generally what they want to do in their life when they grow up. It is not rare that they feel overwhelmed by that frequent asked question and by the approach of these.

However, not only young adolescents have this problem, but also many people with many years of professional experience or unemployed people are affected by such problems. For here too, it must be said that times have changed and that we are now overburdened, for example, by rapid technological progress and the large number of new professions, to decide on a particular profession which we would then like to pursue until retirement or beyond.

Of course, we will not go through all the questions that might be asked, for example via job-finding portals, where in some cases we do not understand the meaning and purpose behind them, in detail. The aim is rather that you discover an awareness for these questions, to crystallize the most important questions for you and to be able to answer them afterwards.

In most cases, children are confronted with an internship for the first time at school and then they have to ask themselves: what do I want to do later anyway? Of course, parents, friends and relatives will tell them about their work in advance, but it has to be a very interesting job to get a child listen carefully and keep the information afterwards. That's why very few of them have developed a clear idea of what they would like to become at this early age. Which, in my opinion, is perfectly fine in this stage of life.

Our two boys were born in the mid 90s and with them I could already clearly see that there had been a career change compared to my time of looking for the right job. Somehow one had the feeling when back then - in my time - the older ones talked about their professions that it was always the same typical ones that you could almost count on two hands. Not only that, some of the narrators had already been working for a single employer for decades and didn't even think about doing anything else or changing employers.

In my opinion, the last version alone is rather rare nowadays. If you ask friends, acquaintances or relatives about their profession today, you will often notice that there are now professions that you may never have heard of before. One reason for this could be that some professions may be considered not very good or inferior to others by some people. On a superficial level, such occupations would usually lose out in comparison to occupations for which training, studies or further qualifications are required.

However, all occupations are part of a whole and should be considered by everybody this way and be accordingly accepted and respected. It should not matter whether someone is in a supposedly "simple" profession.

Working life as a whole, as well as within a company, is made up of many different professions and fields of activity, and should rather be seen as the typical cogwheel that has to mesh together in order to run smoothly. It is therefore important to realise that each activity has a specific value and should therefore be respected. Ideally, the activity should be carried out by people who feel called to this profession or by whom enjoy doing it and not by those who feel forced to do it or do not like what they do at all.

Statistically speaking, since 1971 we only have had almost half of the recognised apprenticeship occupations in Germany, which means that there were actually more different occupations to choose from when I started looking for them at the end of the 1980s. Despite this fact, I still had the impression at the time that the people around me were all only pursuing a handful of specific occupations. This may be due to the fact that at that time we had no Internet search engines and in general fewer platforms on which the individual (exotic and new) training opportunities were presented in detail. We have approximately 330 recognised training occupations that we could learn. Although we can visit various internet search engines and many social media portals, among other things, in order to obtain information on all kinds of subjects today, it seems to become more and more difficult to find a suitable profession for us. Perhaps it is due to a stimulus satiation that overwhelms us.

In the past, if you asked boys what they wanted to be when they grew up, you would get answers like fireman, policeman or racing driver, for girls it was professions like veterinary surgeon, educator or nurse. If you ask the boys today, they rather name professions where you can earn a lot of money. For instance, professional footballer or YouTube star. But it has been proven that girls are also increasingly looking for recognition, good money (this striving is probably due to the long fought for emancipation and the feminist movement) and sometimes tend to professions such as model or influencer. There are still some children who remain faithful to the old traditional professions, but already at a young age many of those as well know about some of the new professions, with which one can possibly earn money easily. Which may also be due to the fact that especially in the social media sector, a lot of young people bustle around and look for their opportunities. You sometimes hear of an easy start and the high earning potential even in your own family, when it comes to the topic of social media.

I have often heard and read that many people do not earlier than in their mid-twenties know, what they want to become. So how can you support a job seeker in finding a suitable profession for him or her?

Internship part 1

When I had to look for my first internship position, I didn't have an actual idea - as probably many other people - of my future profession or how I wanted to earn my money with later. Although I had liked to work with computers and had already programmed smaller programs, the IT professions were too far away for me at that time. I didn't feel that there was any information that would have really reached me, for example, where I could get the opportunity to do an apprenticeship as a software developer.

Apart from my great interest in IT, I was also talented in craftsmanship and could therefore imagine a craft profession for me very well. But maybe you come to this decision too quickly, because you know many professions in this direction or you have heard about these professions a hundred times before. After a two-week internship as an electrician, it was clear to me that this is not really something I can imagine as a future profession for me. I don't mean the craft profession in general, but simply the activity as an electrician. Even though it is frustrating sometimes, being able to exclude something should be considered as a huge success.

When I was in school, we didn't have as many school internships as we have today, even though this would have been very good for some students to find a suitable profession or at least to be able to exclude a supposedly interesting profession. In spite of the theoretical information available today from all accessible sources, the real knowledge often only takes place after it has been put into practice. Many things sound very positive or even very negative in theory and we decide on a certain path based on this theoretical level and knowledge.

Our children today have several school internships in order to be able to make a timely effort to find out what they want to become later. In my opinion this is a good thing and should be appreciated.

Sometimes these internships are rather seen as lucky coincidences that make possible that you do not have to go to school for one or two weeks, which I can partly understand. We have never forced our children to try out certain professions and always left them free to decide what they would like to become later. Our support was more in the direction of recognizing their own strengths and weaknesses and bringing out their current interests.

Our eldest son already had the clear idea of becoming a gardener in his young years. The only complicated thing was that he was allergic and asthmatic and therefore the combination had to be viewed somewhat critically.

Therefore, he decided to try something else and chose a handicraft business in the field of door and window construction. After the internship it was clear to him that it was nothing he could imagine in the long run, but at least he had gained this insight and that is important. Since there was a good remuneration for the internship in this company, our second son decided to come to this company as well and to do his first school internship there. Maybe that should not be the prior criteria, but why not - sometimes you start something on a whim and after a while you notice, oops, I've never thought of anything like this before but the activity suits me perfectly and is fun as well. The first internship primary offers a good first impression of what it can be like in later working life. You can observe the stress level on the basis of stressed out employees there and get a good impression of the variety, the intensity, the possibilities and promotion chances that the job brings along.

Our daughter, who was born in 2000, has a preference for professions that either involve teaching or retail sales. Therefore, she decided to do her first internship in a retail store. The knowledge gained from this was a valuable experience that she always included in the further search for a suitable profession in the future.

The good thing (can be bad as well) about today's world is that sometimes interns are used as cheap and sometimes full-fledged employees. This can be an excellent way to gain practical experience under real stress conditions, even though it can be definitely exploitative as well. Carrying and moving a lot of packages around all day can be a hard burden. Our daughter was able to imagine a career in sales after her internship, but stowing particularly heavy products brought a bitter taste with it.

No matter what your intentions are, I would always recommend trying out a job, since it will always serve as a reference model and can be compared with the other experiences you will have. Not only the comparison will become important, but also a constant mental expansion, which will be composed of all the findings.

Internship part 2

My second internship was either too long ago or I really hadn't had one, because I can't remember it for the life of me- maybe I was sick during that time. That probably fits to the widespread saying: "we had nothing back then, so we are glad that we were allowed to do at least one".

After our children's internship and in preparation for what was to come, we tried to advise them on how they could narrow down and optimise their search for a suitable profession. What should be decisive when choosing a profession is that the job should be fun and that you should at least earn enough to be satisfied. Of course, it is also important to have a good employer, a good boss, great colleagues and a good working atmosphere. For the search, however, these are variables that you cannot necessarily take into account.

Soberly considered, I am looking for a job that I can afford my living with. If I have learned a profession or am doing a job I enjoy, I can exchange the remaining variables, such as a great environment. However, if I already have a job that I don't enjoy, the great environment with boss and colleagues will only help me to a limited extent and should not be a permanent solution. Activities or jobs that are no fun at all make you sick in the long run.

It will be noteworthy easier for you to orientate yourself afterwards, because if you know that you enjoy your current job, but not in your current workplace, then you only have to change your environment. But it could just as well be that at some point my profession, which I loved in the past, just isn't fun anymore to me. Then I better start something else, because even if the environment fits, but my job/activity is no longer fun, I have to change this component, otherwise it will make me unhappy.

On the one hand, I suggest you to include only a few criteria regarding you search, but on the other hand you will come across some criteria in the course of the book which could become important for you and which should also be included. When I speak of few criteria here, then only when it comes to the sober consideration: "I am looking for an activity that suits me and with which I can make a living". All criteria that are necessary to finally define the fields of activity that really suit me and that I could enjoy in the longer term are of course included. That means that, depending on your priorities, these criteria can be a lot after all.

In order to define the criteria that are important to you, you have to break everything down a bit further, so that you can filter, exclude or narrow down the selection options more easily.

In many professions there is already a restriction by the school qualification and therefore this is an important indicator for you to make further decisions. In order to have the best possible chances to choose a profession of your own choice, you often need to have a high school diploma. This way is unthinkable for many people, although they often have what it takes. For others it is not possible because they would be overwhelmed by the demands of school.

One of our sons switched to the grammar school (in German "Gymnasium") from the fifth grade onwards (after primary school in Germany), as he certainly had what it takes. Many topics flew to him and he learned the most important things already during the actual lessons, but he was not willing to do more out of class. Therefore, he could not deliver the same performances as his classmates and was unfortunately very difficult to motivate to do more for the school. It came after two years, as it had to come. The lightness and his great advantage of learning fast had been too little in the long run to keep up a good grade point average and to compensate for the higher demands. As we know, grades are an important criterion on which a personnel officer bases his or her decision whether the applicant has sufficient or even the best qualifications in the most important subjects for the choice of career.

Our son was placed from the gymnasium to the German "Realschule" which is similar to the secondary school and had also achieved his good grade point average again. The knowledge of many learning units shows: People with learning disabilities are difficult or sometimes even impossible to teach. Here the minimum - maximum principle is used, which is the attempt to achieve the best result with minimum effort. The will is decisive, which means that even though the potential is there, it always depends on whether the person is ready for an additional performance. In any case, I can definitely say that he regrets today that he has not provided the additional service although he could have done it easily, regarding his intellect. Such a degree can always be made up for, but it doesn't get any easier the older you get and the more dependencies you have suddenly developed around you. Partner, children, job-related work combined with going to night school is not easy - so think about the fact whether you are said to have what it takes, because then I can only recommend: do something with it (immediately).

Since we as parents don't want to define any status symbols to our children, it didn't matter to us if the child doesn't attend a secondary school and graduate from high school. So, if you think it is important for your children to have a good school career, you should always observe and remember that school, learning, classmates and teachers can bring a high stress potential with them, which can also have negative effects. Our son was much more relaxed, less stressed and happier what is the most important thing for us as parents. Try to make sure that it is mainly positive stress and that challenges should be there, but not in a too large amount.

The second internship of this child was as a baker in a family business. This was a concrete profession wish he could imagine. The internship lasted two weeks and was exhausting for him, just by getting up early. He enjoyed the job, but it was still clear to him that he did not want to work this early in the day.

Our daughter decided to do her second internship in a primary school. Here she was allowed to accompany various teachers in their teaching activities and in some cases to actively involve herself in the lessons. She was also able to gain an insight into the remedial classes for a while, as the teachers needed help there. Therefore, she could draw very instructive conclusions after this internship. For example, she partly enjoyed teaching in the area of primary school, but children can be very demanding at that age. So, she concluded that if she decided for a pedagogical profession, she would rather choose to teach in secondary school or high school.

It becomes clear that in order to create a suitable search filter for you, there are a few things to consider. Which things are the most important for you personally, you have to figure out by yourself after all.

It is important that you are as honest as possible with yourself. Most people know these typical websites where you can find suitable professions for yourself. But our children and many others, too, cannot identify with the end result, because they usually provide very abstract results, especially for the small amount of questions. I have done these tests uncountable times and the result is often something I can't really imagine. It is noticeable that you hear of this experience a lot from others as well.

These programs indeed can be good decision makers, but often they are not broken down in detail so far that everyone can easily get along with the questions and especially with the result occupation, or one has not yet found complete criteria for oneself. So, it feels like everything starts all over again and everything is stuck to you again.

Children, especially in the puberty phase, have a way of doing things, where everything depends on how things are specifically named. During that phase it can often happen that one expects something from a child, but does not choose the wording that the child expects or wants to hear. Therefore, it is incredibly difficult especially for such rigid programs to find clear ways and names to describe some processes understandable, so that everyone can use them.

This means that again the parents or helpers, who form the dictionary between the outside world and the pubescent child, are needed. Children learn about many different topics at school, but often with little practical relevance, regarding the current time.

If you take a look at some of the questions mentioned above as a parent, you will quickly realize that even though we learned and acquired knowledge by ourselves and have more experience in life, but still cannot cope with some of these questions, as many of them are ambiguous. Therefore, it is inevitable that everyone refines his search mask for himself, even with his own words. Adults should also not be afraid to ask for help if they cannot cope with the questions.

What could be important criteria?

What could be such criteria and how can I define them for myself? As a tip: Start with rough general definitions and questions where you can basically already take a side and then ask yourself the same questions over and over again. As an example: Would I prefer to work **outside or inside**? For all those for whom there is no in-between - for example, there are some consulting professions where you spend part of your time in the office and part of your time in the sales force- you can already sort out some professions here that are no longer suitable for you.

As far as my **school career** is concerned, the higher it is, the more choices I have. If it is clear at an early stage in which professional direction or even in which targeted profession it is going to be, then you know from the outset what schooling this profession requires. However, one should not forget to look beyond the horizon and check which paths I can take with my profession later on. Here you can quickly come to the recognition that there are further qualifications or even further training courses that require a university degree. One could say that I should be primarily guided by the points that are important to me and that I am comfortable with. But here it can very quickly lead to a problem, because one must not forget that many people want to learn a profession for which they have **enthusiasm**. It should be irrespective in some cases of whether this enthusiasm has been there all your life and the amount of experiences you have in this specific area.

It becomes apparent that we also have criteria that we cannot easily measure. For example, the al-ready mentioned degree of experience that one has already gained in the kind of work they could imagine professionally. As an example, I would again mention the football player. There are those who have already played football in their free time and then go to a football club to learn more and/or play football as a team sport. It may be that the coach finds out that the player does play football well and also has an idea about football, but that he probably won't become a huge talent.

In contrast there is the person who has an insane enthusiasm for football - where this comes from is sometimes not known - without having had much experience beforehand. Someone who is enthusiastic also finds it much easier to complete unloved exercises and to learn something new and thus makes very rapid progress in the overall package. It can happen that this enthusiasm also leads to a necessary above average talent and this player matures to world class.

That's why it is difficult and risky to judge in advance and one should not hastily do so. In other words: giving up desired professions for which you have a great interest, just because people think that you gained too little experience so far. It counts a lot if someone has a strong enthusiasm for some-thing and the necessary experience can often be built up bit by bit. Someone who approaches a matter with the greatest enthusiasm and a little talent, will quickly overtake those who only bring initial experience without being really enthusiastic in their work in their learning progress.

So, back to the enthusiasm, as already mentioned, our first son was keen to pursue the profession as a gardener. Therefore, we encouraged him to try out his second internship in a nursery. This internship was around Easter and thus it was during the time our son usually has the biggest allergy problems. A two-week internship is obviously much shorter than an apprenticeship over three years, but it still provides a good basis for getting an overview when it comes to the question of whether one can do the job physically or health-wise. In these few weeks you should ensure that you try to observe your work colleagues and ask them a lot of questions to get an impression of how you might be challenged in this work later. Afterwards you can weigh whether this combination is suitable for you or whether the problems are simply unbearable for you and there-fore would be senseless for you to dedicate yourself to this job. Shortly said, our son found his way around the internship and was still very enthusiastic about this job afterwards. His health problems were within a normal range, just as he always had them during spring time.

Another criterion would be to think about whether one would rather do **mental activities or physical activities**. As already mentioned, the job seeker should define the criteria himself and assess them honestly. Of course, it is helpful to get an assessment, especially from parents, good friends and acquaintances, of how they see you and what type of person you appear to be to them. Fittingly, I would like to say that many people have a huge problem with self-assessment and only very rarely can they assess themselves accurately. The majority are known to tend to underestimate themselves, although there is also the other group, which is likely to overestimate itself on certain important matters. But what does this finally mean for our supposedly honest search? It means that the strengths and weaknesses you have defined for yourself will simply often move in the wrong direction, which of-ten is not a good thing for you as a job seeker. Because what happens to misjudgements? On the basis of these, we form important criteria for us, with which we want to select our profession, and thus we falsify the results in the worst case completely.

If I underestimate myself constantly, then I will per-haps not be able to answer certain questions correctly, because underestimation often leads to great uncertainty and nervousness in the long term. Many people constantly doubt themselves and those doubts will lead to questions like: Am I really able to do that? Does that suit me? And not infrequently one then comes to the conclusion: Oh, I cannot do this at all and I will never be able to do so! In principle, you demotivate yourself until you have classified this question, which is becoming more and more exhausting for you, as negative with a good and relieved conscience and have accordingly taken the easiest way to get rid of it. On the other side, the person who overestimates himself tends to take the asked questions lightly and tries (sometimes desperately) to make himself believe that all this is absolutely no problem for him and that he could do it easily.

That is why it is immensely important as a job seeker to closely listen to the external assessment, to question these afterwards and may ask the assessors: Have I really given you this impression and if so, why?

This is the only way for the job seeker to strengthen his self-assessment, because the more information he gets about self-assessment and external assessment, the better and more accurate he can finally assess himself. In this way the jobseeker is also able to correct his self-assessment upwards or downwards, depending on the information from others. Of course, the rule applies again that you question the received information and reflect on yourself beforehand, because even people close to you can (possibly) misjudge you. By regularly dealing with this topic, you will be better and better able to assess yourself and thus get rid of many uncertain-ties. But what is the point of putting yourself through all that work? The answer to that question is actually quite simple. The more precisely you can assess yourself, the more confidently you will be able to answer the asked questions and even perform in front of important people. Dear overconfident people, if you simply don't want to or cannot admit to the outside world or to yourself that you are not as good in everything as you think, then listen to everything carefully and secretly correct your criteria. Hardly nobody will ask you later, which specific criteria you used to find this exact profession for your-self.

It's not always necessary (but often relieving) to admit your weaknesses to the outside world, but people with job experience will usually find out very quickly if the information you sometimes have to disclose really fits. To know your own weaknesses and to be able to admit them is a strength, you should always be aware of that.

Do I want to **create something?** Here, again, are some activities and professions, which you can easily exclude according to your individual answer. If you can answer this question with a yes for your-self, it does not matter at this point in which field of activity this development should take place. It could range from pottery, to programming or to scientific fields. On the other hand, it is not up to everyone, as some prefer to deal with the finished product, what is perfectly fine.

The great thing is precisely this diversity, which we all bring along individually. It is exactly this diversity that additionally stimulates the creative minds and encourages them to create new fields of activity for all those who have strengths in them or have a great interest in them. As we know, our goal should be to narrow down this huge list so that only those professions and fields of activity remain that match our (current) interests, skills, qualifications and enthusiasm. However, we should not lose ourselves in the ideal of finding a hundred percent match, because there are usually always light and dark sides in every single profession. There will always be things that make you happy, that you enjoy doing and that give you the feeling that you have made the right choice. In contrast, there will always be areas in a profession that you are not comfortable with, that you do not really enjoy and through which you sometimes just have to fight yourself. Balance is key here.

It is absolutely worth mentioning that these unloved areas can also become good or neutral areas for you, which you suddenly do not see as troublemakers anymore. However, this depends on how often you have to deal with them, how much experience you can gain in those activities and how much you are willing to get involved with them and to accept them as much as possible and learn to deal with them. So, don't be discouraged if your profession contains some areas that cause you to feel insecure and make you fear that the effort behind it could be too high. Even if it might turn out that it is not the right profession for you, you will certainly grow with the challenge and be stronger afterwards.

Many areas of activity and topics that you will hear about and learn during the training are always related to the big picture and should be viewed far be-yond the horizon.

In principle, the individual professions have always a similar structure: there are certain basic professions where specialisation in specific core areas follows. This therefore always means that if I learn a profession, I automatically come into contact with the extended specialisations that this profession brings with it.

In the IT world, for example, there are five basic professions that you can learn. These basic professions are then divided into about 30 specialisations. If you are in a company with a small number of employees, you will be able to cover a lot of areas of each specialisation yourself.

In larger companies, these areas are often divided into departments that focus on either one or very few specializations. In smaller companies you therefore learn a variety of things and can build up very good experiences from all specialisation areas. In larger companies with departments and limited fields of activity, you are more likely to acquire detailed and specialised knowledge and can therefore become a specialist in a certain area more quickly.

In these specialisations you will gain the necessary knowledge and the years of work experience to be able to rise to a management position.

In addition to these specializations, there are a few bachelor and master courses of further education in the IT sector, which represent the highest qualification level of the IT professions.

You will find such a structure in many professions and if you have decided on a basic profession, I recommend that you take a look at the further training opportunities as well. This should also answer the (important) question: **What can I do with my profession later on?**

Another indicator for our filtering can be the question of social professions and the accompanying question: Do I want to **help other people with my job?** As I said, even a generalisation is enough to make it clear for yourself whether you want to or do not want to do this. Many people automatically as-sociate social professions with nursing professions, but it is perfectly possible to be socially involved in different ways and in other jobs. This is more about the rough general direction of interests that you have.

For example, as a clerk in aid organisations I also contribute with my work to help other people, even if it is perhaps a less active way to do so. A clear recommendation on my part would be to first filter this area in general. Later on, you can see in the remaining selection whether you would like to help people with distance or directly. Here, of course, it is also the case that there is no such thing as only black or only white. There are also the intermediate solutions where you can combine both.

Computer activity or not? Especially in today's time it is hard to imagine life without computers, but there are also professions that can still be done without or with little computer use. There are some among us who say that they cannot cope with a computer or at least not well enough for them to imagine it on a daily basis. Or even people who, in principle, cannot imagine sitting on an office chair all day. In this case too, there are wonderful combination solutions that enable you to combine office work with field work and, in some cases, also give you the opportunity to work in your home office.

The home office area is exciting for many people, but can turn out to be an intensive time guzzler. It is not unusual, once you have spread out your work in your home environment, for you to pass by your work area again and again and decide to do some-thing "quickly" after all, even if you had actually decided to call it a day. Therefore, we tend to spend more working time in the home office than we would spend in the office. Although the home office indeed has its advantages, it is important to set yourself limits again and again so as not to overtax yourself.

Back to my children: Our garden-loving son was on the verge of making his next move and decided to do an internship in a kindergarten as an educator. As stated in the beginning, we do not try to push our children into a certain profession, but rather try to show them the possibilities and let them choose their own paths. That is why we have encouraged our children to look at and try out different jobs. Trying several things out helps us to get a better feeling for whether the activity could really be some-thing for us as well as comparing the different experiences afterwards. In theory, you can acquire a lot of knowledge and learn much about a profession beforehand. However, it is possible that sometimes you suddenly catch yourself and realise that every-thing sounded perfectly fine in theory, but it feels completely different in practice. So, it can be said that practical experience is often underrated and is definitely worth a try if you are interested in a certain profession.

Do I want to wear uniforms? For some people it is out of question to do so, because it makes them feel constricted and uncomfortable.

Try to define your personal preferences regarding that matter and keep in mind which possible consequences a general yes or no decision might have for you.

In many companies, even on a small scale, wearing uniforms is required for image purposes or self-image. These uniforms sometimes just consist of simple things, such as t-shirts or caps. And remember that we always start from the here and now! If you are looking for a profession or an activity at the present moment, then obviously the current position you have on things is decisive. If you realize in the course of your activity that you could achieve more and you could imagine a position in the management or something similar, you will rarely get around a certain dress code.

The majority of people change their clothing style often in their lives. In younger years the clothing style is usually more casual and the older you get, the less of the former style retains in many cases. However, there are always some who like to continue wearing a more youthful style that makes them feel younger and fresher. Still, this is, of course, something that everyone has to decide on their own, so I recommend to handle this matter as all the other advices and criteria. After all, your decisions and ideas have to suit you, as they should stimulate your thoughts and ideally have a pioneering effect on you. Yet, this does not mean that there will only be these paths imagined by you, because everything only happens in your head. You establish the basis through your ideas and in the best case you will receive a virtual signpost at every virtual fork, which can show you the possible paths you have imagined and decided on, based on your preferences and criteria.

Exactly here lies the biggest sticking point. Namely, when I know my preferences and my criteria, but feel like I have already seen and tried out all the signs of the virtual signpost. What next? Firstly, you should always take care not to be at a standstill, because especially today everything is constantly changing - some things rapidly and others very slowly.

So, it can always happen that you either take some paths too early or too late. Do not worry, just be-cause a path has failed does not mean that every-thing has been in vain. Here you should ask your-self why this happened and whether you would have had influence on it or maybe still have and then you should either learn from it or change something if necessary. Thomas Edison is supposed to have said symbolically: "I haven't failed, I've just found 10.000 ways that won't work". So, do not get discouraged and rather try to expand your ways, because what is stopping you from going new ways?

You should keep in mind that there are very good alternatives for all activities, where the already ac-quired experience can be used very well. It is important to come to the realization that there is more for you elsewhere and that you have the courage to change something.

In my opinion, people should learn to rethink and become more versatile. If, for example, I can no longer do my job for health reasons, I still have the valuable experience I gained. In addition to that, if I can no longer do the job physically, I can think about what I can do with my knowledge instead.

Is it possible to do the "same" activity with less stress? Sometimes it is sufficient to change the employer in order to get a significant relief here. Unfortunately, this is not enough sometimes and therefore the considerations have to continue: what can I do now? I would suggest to look for existing parallels and to estimate your personal value, be-cause, for instance, someone who has been in the profession for a few years is in many cases an ex-pert in his field or subfield. Often the bridge can be built here, for example, instead of being an executive person as before, one can consider moving to a desk. This means that you are able to let the valuable experience flow into your "new" activity and to keep the good feeling that you can continue your job, not as once intended, but at least in a different form.

This type of change is welcomed by many companies, as they are able to maintain an employee, who has the necessary understanding of the previous activity, in their company. The employee knows ex-actly how the work process of the last activity is go-ing and he is aware of the time units and the work-loads and can therefore very well carry out the new planning for the former work area.

So, do not be afraid to rethink and to get to know old things in a new way, as it can be surprisingly refreshing and relieving.

While your signpost may only show two or three directions at the beginning, it is possible to create some more branches with regular reflection and readjustment.

Which **physical "permanent posture"** is important to me?

Of course, we are all different and not everyone is able to sit or stand permanently. What about working at height or underground? Under water, in the laboratory or in weightlessness?

Use your signposts again and try to classify your possible activities in a new way over and over. It is possible that you have to write down your findings in the beginning, but you will notice that after several phases of consideration you will be able to keep your valences very well. Additionally, it will not present a problem anymore to call them up at short notice if necessary. If I have already either discovered or excluded possible ways for me, then I am automatically able to classify short-term offers faster. In addition to that, if you know what you want, you know your junctions and are quickly able to place the new sign, remove it or mark it as a dead end if necessary.

For example, imagine getting the offer to take over a certain position and you also know the activities that are behind it. In your head the answers could be: "Yes", "No", but also "sounds interesting, I could expand my career with this opportunity."

Do I want to work with **foreign languages**? You should be able to individually rearrange, clarify and extend the asked questions for your understanding. Many questions, just like the current one, are very general formulated. So, you should constantly find new ways to expand your personal interests as well as the resulting activities of them. Typically, many people tend to limit the foreign language field almost exclusively to pure interpreting activities, in form of written documents or in verbal form.

In this day and age, however, it must be said that in many professions it is becoming very important to speak a foreign language (fluently), especially business language. One reason for this may be that there are also some foreign-language companies that are setting up in Germany or have already done it. On the other hand, German companies are also striving for an international expansion in order to be able to operate worldwide.

It becomes clear by now that it is indeed not adequate to say that this area is clearly and merely assigned to interpreting.

In some activities or professions, it is sufficient to have at least a certain basic understanding to be able to communicate with customers or business partners within the company. Of course, some companies already offer foreign language courses, which you can often join for free. You should therefore decide whether you would like to have to do with foreign languages, in whatever form. You should consider if it should suffice for a short mediation or a small consultation or rather for an all-round service, where you should not only be able to speak the (business) foreign language fluently, but also be able to write it. In some professions you will find significantly good entry opportunities, the more foreign languages you are able to speak. In some areas this has little or nothing to do with the international businesses, but rather with the customers.

For example, if you had aspired to become a banker in the mid-1980s, your foreign language skills were not particularly required and you did not necessarily have to bring any. Nowadays, this has changed tremendously in this profession as well as in many others.

Many people of different nationalities live in Germany and therefore speak different languages. These private persons as well as, for example, politicians receive visitors from the surrounding foreign-language countries or the whole world.

For these visitors the bank is an important contact point. Nowadays, banking matters are mainly handled digitally or via ATMs, but a visit to the bank counter is still necessary for many people.

It is therefore not surprising that the search for employees that are able to speak several foreign languages has become increasingly important in this profession, as well as in many others. Job offers with the words "it is advantageous if you can speak another language in addition to German and English" were increasingly frequent. In my opinion, this phenomenon is declining again in the bank sector due to the fact that most banks are trying to keep counter services to a minimum, as far as possible. Of course, advisory appointments for account openings or similar matters are still being held, as personal advice is still indispensable in many areas as well as for many customers. However, it is eye-catching that many services can already be purchased online and that many potential customers are increasingly looking for a preferably uncomplicated solution to purchase something. Therefore, I personally think that there is a strong tendency to-wards online services, for instance, webinars in the new media. Another example is that if a customer would like to receive personal advices in the future, these will be provided online somehow.

So, think about how and if you want to deal with languages in general in your (future) activity or profession. Let's suppose, you are multilingual, but currently you have no interest in using those different languages in your work. Yet, it is a huge advantage for you, because you have the power of decision in the end, as multilingualism is really asked. I won't accuse you of any efficiency loss here- just because you have a certain knowledge, it doesn't automatically mean that you want to use it. And that is perfectly fine! However, keep in mind that if your attitudes and priorities change, you will have additional opportunities to look for new professions due to your foreign languages. During all these considerations you should always reflect on yourself and try to define your strengths in an exact way.

Maybe you also have a **creative streak**- can you easily entertain the people around you, are you the joker for everyone or the good narrator or even the one who can easily fool others? Many people quickly say that they are not really good at anything or that they are not really interested in anything. You should therefore define the things you are known for and how you see yourself. Let yourself be assessed by others on this matter as well - what impression do the others have? If someone is able to make family, friends, acquaintances and even strangers laugh easily and still has fun by oneself and feel good about it, then this person should con-sider doing an activity in this area. Although people like to be entertained and are also looking for fun, they are often very demanding. "Working where other people go on vacation", that would probably be a dream for many people. Obviously, there can and will be stony paths, as in any profession, because it is not easy to entertain a demanding audience. All in all, however, it is to be seen as in all professions: If you start a job, then it is often not directly clear at the beginning whether you are really suited for it in the long run. There's no guarantee for that, so I can only advise you to firstly stay firm and not to give up (too quickly), because unfortunately our society has become a throwaway society these days. I have the feeling that we humans have developed the urge to quickly go from one extreme to the other sometimes.

Here is an example from which I think that many of you heard of in a similar way. I am a child of the early seventies, generally more of an observer type, a thinker and an analyst, but I don't think that I realized that in my early years. However, I noticed that I tend to overthink certain matters and that I acquire to think outside the box by and by.

Yet, who is actually interested later on whether you have a so-called innate talent or whether you have an above-average starting position due to hard training. In any case, when I looked at some older couples in my circle of acquaintances, I noticed that some of them do not really get along with each other at all. One even had the feeling that they don't really fit together anymore. My friends then report-ed that the elderly woman (in this case) had wanted to get divorced for years. When she was asked why she hadn't done it already, she said: "It would be frowned upon, what would the people say"?

It becomes clear that people were so afraid of gossip and other peoples' opinions at that time, that they preferred not to change anything, no matter how unhappy they were. However, this fear was not only present in this specific field of life, but in principle in all matters where the gossip could spread through the neighbours, through the village and into the neighbouring villages.

In my opinion, some people were almost obsessed with clinging to old traditions. Always with the question in the back of their minds what society would say to a certain decision.

Briefly summarised: many people in the past held on to certain values enormously. Among other things, because they could not tell their opinions aloud without fearing that everyone would point the finger at them. Nowadays, as I had already mentioned, we have become more of a throwaway society. It has never been easier to get rid of things we no longer want. You don't want to continue a contract, just terminate it. I don't want my partner anymore, so I'll just find a new one. The marriage is not going well anymore, then a divorce is the automatic solution. The printer cartridge is empty and as it almost costs as much as a new printer, I have to get a new printer. And, and, and, ... We could add a lot more things to the list, but what I'm trying to tell you is: The fact that it is easier and that supposedly safer for us if we get rid of the "sudden" unwanted things, creates a new problem that should not be underestimated. As we can get rid of partners, objects, work, etcetera so easily, many people lack the necessary ambition to look for other solutions and to fight for the values that used to matter to them. It can be concluded that we have reached the other extreme case, namely: "You don't fit me any-more, I'll exchange you then!" In some cases, this approach is completely acceptable, namely when the situations have been assessed, discussed and countermeasures have been initiated (if necessary) beforehand. If you still have the opinion that it no longer fits or that it makes you unhappy after these considerations, regardless of the matter (work, partner), then sometimes it's better to break away from the old situation and, if necessary, to ex-change it.

I try, if it is possible, to look at things in a sort of Yin and Yang perspective. For those of you who cannot do anything with this: The terms come from Chinese philosophy. As far as I know, the actual meaning is not one hundred percent certain, but for me this is not of greatest importance, because it is about how I and partly also many others understand this symbol individually. One symbol is white and one is black and for me they represent two completely different paths, which actually move in opposite directions, but do not come into conflict with each other, but rather complement each other. I associate this symbol with my personal realisation of a possible middle way, which gives an overview of the existing sides and possibilities. It made me recognise that one can choose an individual middle way and thus is able to choose the best things out of these two sides. There are plenty of Ying and Yang quotations, but mentioning all of them would undoubtedly go beyond the scope of this decision aid. However, I can recommend to research that subject, as it leaves room for interpretations about life and important decisions.

There is one thing I want to warn you about or at least make sure that you keep that matter in mind. In the working world, it is sometimes called "professional tunnel vision"- that is the state that arises when you become more and more the creature of your habits. In other words, this term describes the inability to see beyond the limits of one's own professional agenda. In principle, our brain wants us to become "lazy, but only so far that we have to think as little as possible about whatever things we want to do. Our mind is constantly trying to optimize itself in order to classify and handle recurring tasks more and more easily.

The process of completely acquiring new habits and internalizing them takes us about three weeks. Within this process we learn how to deal with the new habit and to integrate it more and more efficiently into our daily rhythm. After the internalisation and further weeks, months or years, we don't even notice anymore how we approach the habit and how we work off what we have learned. Thus, we no longer have to think about it, we carry out the pro-cesses automatically instead.

If you have already had a longer professional experience and should start a new job or ask friends and acquaintances how some work processes work in their job, you will notice that you recognize possible stumbling blocks of these processes much faster.

If you then ask your colleagues why a certain pro-cess is done in exactly this, perhaps complicated, way, you will often only hear the answer: "I don't know, we've always done it this way." When you set up a company and carry out the first processes, you will certainly have a clear idea of the steps to be taken and what these steps should look like in practice. Since it is not unusual that one cannot al-ways be prepared for all eventualities, let alone plan the processes accordingly in advance, solutions must be created as quickly as possible in that cases.

The question is what happens when these new circumstances are no longer isolated cases and the company has to incorporate the actions into the current system at additional cost. The once run-smoothly system may stumble, as these innovations often can neither be readily nor easily implemented anymore.

The company has to keep running, which means that the solutions have to be adapted quickly, to customer satisfaction and as cost-effectively as possible. Therefore, the company is almost forced to bend and to adapt to these new circumstances. The company has been on the market for a long time, but has now made the adjustments for the majority of process problems. Since these adjustments usually have to be made during ongoing operations, there is little time to consider all eventualities that affect this changeover internally. The new processes are primarily designed to keep the relationship between the customers and the company running. In the meantime, however, it is possible that internal processes take on completely abstruse forms across departments. Additionally, some colleagues could suddenly be dependent on special things in order to be able to manage their working processes.

The result is that simple things suddenly have to be carried out in a complicated way to make everything else work. Unfortunately, it is not that easy to optimize this problem at this point, as there is the question: where do you even start in order not to disturb the recently made processes? In order to not disturb any processes and simultaneously implement the optimizations, you would have to know every little detail internally, as well as the effects on it. In the end, it is no longer possible to change some-thing here without having to take the whole con-struct apart completely. So, it can be said that complicated processes remain in many cases, only in other places.

At least, I would like to awaken in you the consciousness to always stay alert and not to have blinders on. And here I refer to your own blindness, which you can have an influence on. Once you are able to recognize that you might be routine-blinded or on the brink of it, you have the power to change the course of events, before one makes some things just out of habit and no longer with a necessary passion and joy.

Get on with it, try to filter the possible ways and as an interface get the best out of them. Don't give up too soon and see if it is worthwhile for you to fight in order to bring about change. However, try to recognise early enough if it still makes sense!

Awakened consciousness?

Is **working abroad** an option for me? This question should also be considered, as there is a high de-mand abroad, especially for German training occupations. We are ahead of some countries thanks to our detailed and perennial trainings. That's why skilled workers, who have learned in Germany, are very welcome and have the opportunity to find some very interesting professional activities abroad, which are much harder to get in Germany.

In addition to that, experience abroad is always a good thing on your CV and is a good prerequisite if you want to apply for a job in a large company afterwards.

If you not only take the DACH countries, namely Germany, Austria and Switzerland, in account where you don't have to learn a new foreign language, except for the different dialects which we have in Germany as well, then it should obviously fit your language skills in the foreign language area.

Don't forget in your search that you always consider your learning ability. The level of the ability is completely different for each person, but of course you can continue to work on your strengths or weaknesses that you currently have. With diligence and constant repetition, it is likely that certain skills will strengthen.

On the other hand, it can happen at some point, even with diligence, that we reach the maximum where there seems to be no noticeable improvement. Additionally, these learned abilities can also weaken again if you do not have regular contact with them.

Imagine you are doing your favourite sport or some-thing similar. As long as you practice and train it, you will continue improving your skills to a point where they are at their maximum.

Yet, this maximum can also be surpassed by new insights, for example when you get a new coach or change your club and a certain rethinking process takes place. Yes, working life is like a training and there probably will be a point when you notice that you cannot learn earth-shattering new things at work. Of course, this does not apply to all activities with the same intensity, because there are areas and professions that always have to keep up with the latest rights and news. Therefore, they are al-ways in a learning process to take up the news again.

Back to our training and the unlearning of knowledge and skills. As you can imagine, if you do not periodically practice your sport and the exercises it contains, then an insidious forgetting takes place. For instance, if you don't speak a foreign language regularly anymore, then you will partly forget the words and, in the worst case, you have to learn the language again almost from scratch or at least refresh them strongly. This, however, depends on how intensively we had learned the language before. In principle, it is like riding a bike, you don't really forget the process. If you ever have the de-sire to pursue an activity that you once did, then you will need some training time to get up to date, but our brain will remember it more and more and activate the areas that we once used in order to do this specific activity.

Can I keep secrets? In some activities it is necessary to keep secrets to ensure the highest level of security. Whether this possibly only refers to data security or objects, persons and other things is completely irrelevant. Not only the temptation to pass the explosive information, but of course also the psychological pressure behind it should not bother you. So, the question is not only whether you can, but also whether you want to, because it is clear that there will be certain systems, depending on the employer, which you have to go through constantly. It is not an activity for everyone to pass personal information, let alone hiding it, including from their own partner. Among other things, there is the threat of penalty payments of considerable amounts if you do not comply with the obligation of secrecy.

Do you like **to speak in front of others or groups** in general?

Remember that even the wish would firstly be sufficient! In addition to that you should consider it, even if you haven't had so much experience in it. At school you often learn how to speak in front of a group during presentations and speeches. I can only recommend to use these opportunities to build up your self-confidence and to be able to decide whether you could imagine such a thing in your future profession or not. However, you should be aware that this can definitively change the older you get. For instance, many people would probably compare presentations in school with torture, but may enjoy sharing their knowledge with other people later on.

You will see that it will become easier every time if you practice it regularly. Dry runs alone in front of the mirror are a good way to observe yourself and to improve your timing and time management. Furthermore, try to choose a topic in the dry runs that really interest you and in which you already have a lot of knowledge. I recommend that, because at work, too, you will be demanded to talk about topics that you know and have learned. If you have to present a monthly report, how the numbers have changed, for example, the core of the topic always remains the same, in this case the presentation of the sales figures of the month. So, we know that for this specific preparation we have to replace the current values and, if necessary, define where they come from. The procedure remains the same, so practice makes perfect.

Don't worry, even at work you won't get your head torn off right away if the first presentations are a bit bumpy. When you are reminiscing about school, or are still actively involved, you probably have noticed that only few people really feel comfortable speaking in front of the group, especially if it is the first presentation you have ever prepared and given. Just because you get older and already have a job, it does not change from one day to the next.

Can I imagine **working in shifts**? Some years ago, I have worked for about one and a half years in a three-shift system with 24-hour coverage. This means that there has been an operating shift at any time, so there was no temporal idle. My experience is that especially the night shifts can be really exhausting, as the daily rhythm is completely changed. Therefore, in that form this would no longer be an option for me personally.

Yet, there are certainly people who have been working in shifts for several years with pleasure. Here applies the rule again: Everyone should form his own opinion. If you can rule it out for you from the beginning, that's fine. And if not, you should consider it and possibly try it out.

Can I get used to **strong cleanliness and hygiene**? The classic examples are doctors' surgeries, hospitals and the like. Most people are willing to keep a certain basic order, but in these fields of activity it is essential that cleanliness has a particular high priority. Thus, you should think about whether you can imagine this with all the existing consequences, be-cause for some people the smell alone is so problematic that they cannot imagine it. However, re-member not to overestimate the whole thing, as it does not mean that you are automatically not able to start any activity in the field at all.

In hospitals, too, there are very distinct occupational groups, even in administration alone, who do not work in the extreme areas with tightened hygiene regulations. Ergo, a job in a hospital, for instance, is very well possible without having to put on protective clothing or coming in frequent contact with hygiene necessities.

Which **materials** can/would I like to work with? If you already have one or more preferences here, you can include them in your personal criteria. However, it is important to also take your possible previous health problems into account, not only regarding this question but all of the mentioned ones. For in-stance, you will mostly come into contact with wood dust, despite modern exhaust systems in a joinery. Therefore, it would be critical in this case if you al-ready have respiratory problems. If you only have slight complaints, you can still consider doing an internship in the area to get an idea of how you would cope with the strain (example: my son, as explained above). Of course, these restrictions then only apply to those activities that involve direct contact with the materials. For example, if you are considering a craft profession, then you can already exclude or filter out some things by the choice of materials.

In addition to that I can give you the tip to touch the materials - but please no hazardous sub-stances - as it already gives you a first impression. As usual, I want to encourage you to check your preferences and then decide whether you want to work with cold steel, for example, or whether you prefer to work with wood. The general area of mate-rials is not only interesting for those of you who want to deal with the pure processing and possible new creations from the materials, but also for professions that deal with this material in general.

If my interest leads me to wood, then I can also become a forester and take care of the woods among other things. It becomes clear that I don't have to build a table out of the tree right away. Just as well, pure logistics companies can be potential employers here, so that I can stick to my material. Nowadays, it may well be that someone says that, because of all the plastic waste, they cannot and do not want to dedicate their work to a company that deals with plastic or produces them. The decisions are up to you and as already mentioned, the more criteria you can define for yourself and already classify as positive, negative or neutral, the closer you come to your goal of defining a suitable activity for you. Always try to think a little bit

51

around the corners, to draw parallels and to consider which related activities could be derived from it.

If you take a look at the profession finder portals as mentioned at the beginning and follow the tests to the end, many of them will only have a handful of professions as a result. The big advantage of this is that you do not feel too overwhelmed with the amount of results, but people often complain that they are not really able to do anything with them. Somehow there is often still a lot of dissatisfaction and the question is: Am I only good for this? You should never forget that each of us is good and suitable for so many individual activities and you have to learn how to increase your chances.

Only if you start to think outside the box, you will find that there are still some new fields of activity that you could pursue. I prefer to end up with a list of 50 activities and then break it down further, rather than having a handful of choices that only fit me half-heartedly It can happen that you have a general blockade of thinking. In that case it can really help if you just say goodbye to fixed ideas and let your imagination run wild.

How important it is for me to earn a **lot of money**? For many people this is a really controversial topic in which we are all different, as everyone has his own ideas about values and a life status that he wants to achieve, maintain and further develop. It can be said that a well-paid job can bring consider-able disadvantages with it. For example, a significantly increased work effort and an enormous responsibility.

When others already go home, you are still working or preparing. The high responsibility must be well organized, as your work hardly for-gives mistakes and the pressure is often permanently high to very high. Especially 24/7 on-call duty coupled with the normal eight hours daily dose in the office, are very demanding. If you hardly need any sleep and are looking for a lucrative challenge for a while, you are in good hands in this area. From my own experience I can say that at some point you can hardly get the work out of your head. This is due to the fact that you come home from a stressful day at the office exhausted and basically try to get to bed as soon as possible, because you can be rung out of bed at any time. You can imagine that your private life often falls by the wayside. Of course, not every day is the same and there are also very humane days on which things are going really well. But money is not everything and does not automatically make you happy!

So, if you are interested in such challenges, always try to find a good working dose that still guarantees that you get enough relaxation. A high status and fame can be good sources of money on one hand, but on the other hand they also offer a high potential for stress. Imagine having a good influential position, having a house here and a house there and enjoying financial independence. Such a status sounds nice and tempting, but can bring envy and, among other things, criminal energies from the out-side. Moreover, this status often has to be protect-ed with additional security mechanisms, including all-round protection of people and buildings. Of course, you don't have to see everything in a negative light and some things take their course on which you may not have much influence at all. It is a fact that financial independence and high positions can also entail great risks and also can cause serious psychological problems. Such considerations can/should be taken into account when applying for high-profile positions or when earning a lot of money is a high priority for you.

Are you a **team player or individually stronger?** Teamwork is required in many activities; what do you think about it and how do others rate you? Working in a team primarily means to be a part of an ensemble. Additionally, it means that, depending on the size of the team, there will be many different opinions about the most suitable form to work on a task or subtask. Depending on the size of the team, however, teamwork also means that you may have to subordinate yourself. If you want to be a team player, you have to be able to support others and sometimes drop or significantly lower your own wishes and ideas.

For example, if you practice a team sport, then you can think about the advantages and disadvantages you see for yourself. As a team you win and lose together, regardless of whether the decisive execution was initiated by a team member or an external person, for example the referee. Is it okay for me if I have done my best and still lose? If I keep thinking that I would be better off alone because I would have done things differently and I might not have lost, then I should ask myself: Does the team hinder my development? In every team there are usually very different characters with different skills and competences. Just because things didn't go well at the moment doesn't mean that you can't be a team player in general. Sometimes it is enough to change teams and gain different experiences. If you, however, generally have a hard time in a group, what-ever the tasks might be, you are more the type who will progress faster on your own. In other words, you prefer to not be confronted with the problems that might appear within a group, as you consider them as an additional burden on your work and you can simply concentrate (better) on yourself and your work without those. However, just because you work autonomously does not mean that you cannot ask others for advice when you encounter certain problems and seem to go in circles in your search for solutions.

A loner should also have the strength, despite a desired independence, to seek help from others when needed. Which type you are is completely irrelevant, because there is something for everyone. The difference is always only what choice you have left in your search for a suitable profession or activity. Nevertheless, you should remember that some skills are learnable and just as well the preferences of the individual can change over time. So, it's not uncommon for a former team player to decide that he has enough experience in teamwork for his taste at some point, and would like to prove himself alone now. On the other hand, of course, people who have preferred to work alone in the past may find that they are becoming increasingly able to work with others or suddenly even prefer it. True to the motto: "Tastes can change with time", even if one would not have thought it possible oneself. So, try it out and listen inside yourself, because your experiences and decisions will always open up new perspectives for you. There is no right or wrong, regardless of how long you have had lived the sup-posed preference.

Are you stronger in writing or in expressing yourself orally? Some people are able to express them-selves verbally very well and can therefore choose professions where you have to communicate a lot. It is purely a matter of taste whether you prefer being anonymous in a call centre or have personal conversations. Others can express themselves excellently in writing and should use these strengths for themselves as well. You should ask yourself whether it is easier for you to describe certain things in your own words or whether you can get to the heart of the matter better in writing. If you are the hybrid type who is good at both sides, you will have maximum flexibility in professions.

Are you resilient? Are you able to cope well with things that happen in your environment or are you quickly affected by them? You should think about this question if such requirements are demanded of you as an applicant. Depending on the company and the job, the question of stress can then be more precisely defined.

Do I keep a cool head, even when things get stress-ful around me? Of course, you have to think further and limit the considerations if necessary, because here it always depends on the situation or how resilience is defined in the job. (For example, whether physical or psychological). Concrete examples would be whether you keep a cool head when things get hectic around you and if you are still able to do your job very well in such cases. For many people it is also emotionally too difficult to have to deal with other people's problems all the time at work, for instance, because they maybe carry the problems home with them afterwards and have to think about them constantly. Therefore, it is important to find out your strengths and weaknesses and weigh up in which areas you are resilient and in which intensity and try to make the best of it.

Epilogue

Of course, I hope that all the criteria and suggestions I have given here gave you food for thought on how to optimize your personal search, but there is one thing you should not forget. Our single decisions, the sum of our decisions, as well as our experiences make us the person we are. From this it can be deduced that future decisions will make us the person we will be, and there is no right or wrong in doing so. In the course of your life you will come across points and situations again and again where you will notice that something has changed and that it is no longer as it once was. Firstly, this may not always seem positive, but experience shows that you can often discover advantages afterwards and would not want to change the course of your life even if it was possible.

This change can result from a changed environment, but you must not forget one thing: the more decisions we have made and the more experience we have gained, the more we act accordingly. After all, we are a creature of habit and therefore our brain is always trying to find a pattern to classify recurring things. If we do the same thing for years, our brain knows exactly how to act in these situations.

Therefore, it may well be that although our working environment matches our expectations, we lose more and more the fun in our work and in what our activity demands of us. It may not only be that we lose the fun in the mere activity, but - and what is even more important - in who we have become because of it. I like to call it the lucid intervals and for me these are the few seconds when you might fall from work onto the couch and suddenly be struck by a flash of inspiration. Namely, that it cannot go on like this. You have to learn to listen to your body, because it sends you clear signals when something is not to your liking or when something is not good for you. In working life, a lot is expected of employees and you can quickly feel overwhelmed if you approach things with the wrong kind of ambition or simply keep on working stubbornly without any real goal.

Many people are very stressed at work and this is normal to a certain extent and helps them to optimise their own work processes. It is important to recognize the difference between negative stress and positive stress and to use this knowledge for yourself. Everyone needs familiarization periods, especially if you always have to get used to complex topics with which you have not had much contact so far. So, give yourself time and listen to your body, because there is no point in comparing yourself with others hastily. Everybody has their own strengths and weaknesses and just because others might be able to complete a task faster or get used to it faster than you, you shouldn't feel bad about it. We live in a hectic world and everyone should find suitable indicators for themselves, regarding the search for a profession, which clearly answer the question: Am I still on the right track? - because what good is it to me to continue doing my chosen "dream job" when I clearly notice that it no longer fits!

In the beginning I told you that I have heard from some people who report on how many decades they have been working in a company. However, only in individual cases have the statements of these people gone so far that they (still) enjoy their work. When asked why they don't change anything if they don't enjoy their work anymore, you often hear that they are already too old and that they unfortunately didn't realize it early enough. Additionally, they often fear that no employer would staff them, because they are already too "old".

From such a situation many uncertainties and concerns arise, but health is our most precious wealth, which we should therefore try to keep as long as possible in a very good range. So please always consider (if it concerns you) what this work is really worth to you if it destroys so much of your health and your quality of life over time. I want to emphasize that I don't merely mean hard physical work. An instance for this physical work would be the case that I actually have machines available but often end up carrying the kilos from A to B myself, because it is faster or because I can't keep my schedule otherwise. Our body goes through a lot. Of course, it can learn a lot and can cope with the new stresses, but it does not forget!

Nevertheless, you should never underestimate the consequences of psychological stress and therefore be careful with your mental health as well as with your physical one.

The mental activities and professions, where you are challenged all day long, have to keep many topics in mind and are confronted with plenty of data can quickly get into your psyche.

You should always keep in mind that nowadays it is easier than ever to change professionally. It is no longer important and necessary to find a job that you can do until you retire. More important is to listen to your interests, which are likely to change over time and therefore require change.

Therefore, it is absolutely possible that this year you will start your first job and in five years you may have developed completely different interests that will make you change your mind completely. This means that finding a job should more and more become a snapshot. Of course, you should also have long-term goals and plans, but you should also think about the current time and current interests and in which area you want to work now. Templates and criteria that you have created today can, depending on new insights, experiences and personal circumstances, be totally different the next time, even with a short time gap.

At a young age and without great personal ties and obligations, professions are often combined with worldwide travel activities. If one day you have a partner at your side, sooner or later you will have to rethink your personal priorities, especially when the first offspring is on the road and you want to spend more time with your family.

At first, change happens in the mind, so if you often play with the idea of changing things, you should ask yourself clearly in these moments of light: Why is this coming to my mind right now? What are the reasons for this? Where do these wishes for change suddenly come from? In addition to that, it has to be said that if you ask a thousand people, there will certainly be different opinions about what they have experienced in the same profession. This is obvious, because if 1000 people learn one and the same profession, but in different companies, different experiences in positive and negative form will always arise.

Even though they have chosen the same profession, they will still be trained differently, depending on how their boss, their trainer and their colleagues feed them with knowledge. Moreover, there will be a positive or negative collegiality and then you will partly be able to research completely different experiences in only one profession.

This does not even include the different experiences that everyone has had with customers. Here you will also find out very quickly that you get along much better or worse with one or the other customer compared to another work colleague

In the eighties, nineties and early 2000, so-called job-hoppers, i.e. people who change their job approximately every two years, were not welcome. This is due to the fact that most employers preferred to have a reliable employee for as long as possible. The new employee sometimes has to be trained for months in order to fully understand and master his tasks. The invested energy, time and financial expenses of this endeavour should of course be invested for as long a period as possible.

In the beginning/mid 2000s, however, the companies' view of job-hoppers changed significantly. As I have said before, decisions also provide food for thought and new ideas for employers. Some employers had now decided that job hoppers are very well suited for some of their areas of activity. In some cases, even better than employees who have been working in a company for years. One of the main reasons for this is that a job hopper gets to know different companies and different activities and designs of these. It is always a certain risk for the employer to hire a skilled worker, because he has only limited knowledge - if he not knows the training company - about how the new employee has been trained. Here the employers must also rely on experience and so it is not surprising that some training companies serve as door openers for various larger companies. After all, experience shows that trainees who have learned in a certain company are usually best suited to start a job in it with the least amount of effort. As a job-hopper you get around a lot and you get a lot of experience which the company can use well. As a job-hopper you learn to be incredibly flexible and to adapt quickly to the most diverse circumstances.

Take a relaxed approach and try not to put a label on yourself. We often react to and live according to the fundamental decisions and experiences, that we've been through. This leads to the fact that it sometimes doesn't even seem weird to make decisions that seem incomprehensible to some others.

Here is a kind of small "taste test", which you can simply check in different ways. We are a consumer society and there were already different manufacturers of chocolate in the 80s, but mostly only two or three different flavours. Unlike today where we are almost overwhelmed with the range of products on offer today. An enormous stimulus satiation is taking place here. We ask ourselves the question of taste, how should eggs, for example, taste? And how do we assess this?

Quite simply, we judge it by the different points of contact we have experienced with the eggs. These can be of completely different nature and characteristics. Our brain tries - roughly speaking - to receive incoming stimuli, to evaluate them, to classify them, to update them and to recall them when needed.

So, it is a training effect that leads us to learn to assess things and their effects.

Let us imagine a child growing up in city life and getting eggs in the usual way in the supermarket. The child perceives the egg, i.e. the shape, colour, smell, packaging, taste, etc. The first data is stored in its brain at this point. When this child eats eggs once in a week, there is a constant updating process, because sometimes the packaging may look different, sometimes it is the colour, size or taste. We perceive it and our brain basically forms its own truth about this product, which is adapted to our very personal experiences with it. The child grows up and reliably knows everything about the egg, i.e. where it comes from, how it can be prepared, etc, but of course only in the individual form in which the person has known the egg all his or her life.

Now the meanwhile adult gets to know someone from the country with his own farm, his own cattle and among them chickens. At a dinner invitation he gets a taste of the farmer's eggs and he now receives a new update, but what result this update triggers for him depends on many factors. Usually there is an enormous difference in taste and colour between eggs that have just been laid fresh and then prepared, as opposed to those from the supermarket. So, there can be updates in all directions and most of the time we are so surprised that we primarily think that no egg tastes like this or that we generally just don't like it. The reason for this is that we are used to something different, humans are simply creatures of habit. Probably a test person from the country will have similar concerns when he sees a package from the supermarket. Again, people who are used to both know the subtle differences and can classify the eggs even better. Such tests and many more are available in abundance on the internet.

Another good example are videos about the comparison of ketchup in different colours. It perfectly expresses what an enormous influence and what effects our collected experiences of known things have on our brain and then also on our feelings. Ketchup is so prominent in our memory that many people have trouble accepting it in another colour. In the tests mentioned above, for example, a normal red, a green and a blue ketchup are tasted. The colorants were completely tasteless and the production was otherwise identical. However, many of the test persons actually said that the other colours tasted different as well! Someone who doesn't know ketchup and is presented with a green one, looks at it completely objectively and considers it normal. As can be seen, we are the sum of our decisions and the experience we have gained. So, gather experiences, make decisions and learn about the effects. Try to optimize yourself, even if it might be small steps like changing the way you do a task or the way you look at it.

Every little bit helps you to move forward, for it remains stored in your brain, waiting to be requested. In many areas this is called "dangerous" half-knowledge. Namely, when you heard and read something here and there and simply put the rest together by yourself. Sometimes you hear a keyword and suddenly a thought goes through your head-exactly then an information was just retrieved. Maybe this decision helper will help you in other situations and you will see things from several sides.

Our older son is still happy to work as a landscape gardener and the other one will start an apprenticeship as an industrial clerk this year. The latter is also one of those people who are quite late (late in the sense defined by society) - he is approaching his mid-twenties - in knowing what you want to become. So, I want to encourage you to not give up and free yourself from the thought that you absolutely only have to do one job/activity until you retire. Our daughter developed a great fondness for Great Britain and for the English language. She decided to study "British Studies" combined with German language and literature studies with the option of a teaching profession, in order to be able to work as a teacher later on.

I firmly believe that sooner or later everyone will find the right path and profession for themselves and the motto here is also: "Better late than never!". In this sense, I hope that all readers feel inspired in some way and either have a plan now how to filter out the right profession for themselves or perhaps have found the courage to change something. Sometimes you feel as if you are trapped in a hole, either when you are young and have the feeling that nothing really fits you, or when you are already working and would like to break out of the usual and do something new. It is important to know that you are not alone and that many people feel this way and that impressions from the outside and inside can change a lot about this feeling. Talking to different people about it, reading guidebooks, getting information on the internet and going inside yourself and finding out what you really want and what you can imagine, are only a few tips that you can implement in such a situation. I hope this decision aid was a first step in the right direction.

Thanks a lot for reading!

Job Finder
In search of the right job for me

Index

English edition - Kindl Version
Published in April 2020 on Amazon.
ASIN: B086ZZF8C1

German edition - Kindl Version
Published in March 2020 on Amazon.
ASIN: B086KX8SZJ

German edition - Paperback edition
Published in May 2020 on Amazon.
ISBN: 9798646109485

Job Finder
In search of the right job for me